Published by Crooked Wall Press
Copyright © 2022 Jarod K. Anderson
All rights reserved
ISBN: 9798826128046

Cover Illustration: Pin oak (Quercus palustris) from the Meyers
Konversations-Lexikon 1897

Love Notes from the Hollow Tree

Jarod K. Anderson

Author's Note:

Thank you for being here.

This is my second collection of poetry. My first collection *Field Guide to the Haunted Forest* sparked an amazing outpouring of love and support that enriched my life in myriad ways. I am sincerely grateful.

In the introduction to my first collection, I said that much of the contents therein strayed from what I would traditionally call poetry. That remains true in these pages. I include scraps of prose and the germ of larger thoughts. I include bits of daydreams and outright silliness. I counted at least two dad jokes.

I have shaken the urge to apologize for the unusual nature of these collections.
I have eclectic interests, a stormy mind, and a need to write plainly and honestly.

I think the form of these collections is honest.
The structure of these books reflects my ADHD coupled with the highs and lows of my lifelong struggles with chronic depression. Perhaps most of all, these collections reflect my stubborn efforts to stay positive and celebrate kindness, both the willful kindness of people and the intrinsic kindness of nature.

All I can promise is that the words and ideas in this book felt worthy to me. I hope you find them to be worthy too.

Jarod K. Anderson
Delaware, Ohio
April, 2022

Thank you to Leslie J. Anderson, a wonderful poet, editor, and partner.

Thank you to the odd, lovely community who supports my writing and podcasting on Patreon.
Patreon.com/CryptoNaturalist

I couldn't do it without you.

Welcome

Step inside my cabin and hang your coat by the door.
You smell of snowfall and hemlock boughs.
I just fed the stove and the logs are whispering like radio static.
Soon, that white lace on your boots will pool on the floorboards,
making them shine like polished stone.
Rest here as long as you like.
It's no trouble that our meeting place is imaginary.
Many worthwhile things are.

Sting

To feel both utter frustration
and unqualified love for the world is the tension I'm learning to endure.

That feeling is the constant, crackling fire within my skull
and I am forever shutting my eyes against its stinging smoke,

while reaching toward its warm glow.

Cauldron

One day,
your skull will be as empty as a conch shell on a fence post,
full of wind and gentle quiet.

Today,
it's a cauldron of ghosts.
Flesh and electricity.
Water and memory.
A machine that makes reality.

Now.
Here.
Your skull is the garden where fact flowers
into meaning.

Bright

If I can hand you, a stranger, a bundle of words
like warm bread wrapped in cloth,
then this world can't be all bad.

Shelter

Often, my mental health does not cooperate with my creative goals.

Often, "does not cooperate" is an understatement.

I frame this as "brain weather."

Sudden snow may disrupt my gardening plans,
but the snow is not being malicious.

It's not my enemy.
It's just the weather.

During my decades of storms,
I have found that I can strengthen my shelters
and sharpen my forecasts,
but I still don't steer the clouds.

I find this metaphor helpful.

Natural hardships aren't punishments.
Nor do we own them.

So, we should not blame ourselves for our struggles
to stay warm and dry.

Zoom #1

Thanks for joining this Zoom call.

I know it's a Friday afternoon,
so I'll try to be brief.

A couple things about me.

I think the best things come in "clumps."

My skin is the stretched pink sky of a dawnless inner bog
full of hooting owls and hungry mud.

I wish to sleep for another 1,000 years,
but, deadlines, amiright?

How Much?

Your favorite song does not use all notes simultaneously.
Your favorite art is not all shades and hues.
The sweetness in life is as much a question of omission as inclusion.
Remember this when considering your own limitations.
The answer to "what is enough?" is not "all of it."

Getting Dressed

Today,
you may be as natural as a new leaf unfolding in silent softness above
a river valley.

Tomorrow,
you may be as natural as the crushing deep of the ocean floor,
where darkness is a clenched fist.

Choose the nature you need for the day you face.
Wear it well.

Cartographer

When we are born,
we arrive on the shores of a wilderness —
our minds.

We search for shelter.
We tumble into ravines.
We taste the berries that nourish and the ones that leave us
delirious in the mud.

All our lives we struggle to find footing in the forests of ourselves.
There are strange hills inside our thoughts.
Slowly, through messy effort, we become
native to these inner landscapes.

Don't be ashamed
of your stumbles, your scars, your sleepless nights.
You are here.
Wild and whole.

Learning to map the clouds.

Open Secret

Everyone has a story.
With a castle.
And a lady in white.
And children who smile at the space over your shoulder.
And the old stone well.
And a clockface on the moon.
And blue lights above the swamp.
And the smell of cellar soil in her hair.
Everyone has that same story.
We're just too polite to discuss it.

When All Else Fails

I have to assume that in the fullness of time,
at least once,
a mouse has used a mushroom as an umbrella.

I think, today,
that's enough to keep me going.

Could Be

There is so much that might exist,
but doesn't.

I feel the gulf between words and meaning,
so vast it empties me to consider.

There.
Now.

The universe has shifted and there's a moth wing at its center,
gray as ash.

Now again.

A dandelion seed tumbling skyward.

And we all tumble with it.

An Emerald Heaven

I hope there is life elsewhere in the universe.

I don't care about aliens and advanced technology.
I just want one planet that is all moss.
A perfect sphere of soft, green carpet.

I hope it exists and that no human foot ever dents its plush,
perfect surface.

Book of Earth

Stone writes the best eulogies.

Seashells pressed like flowers between pages of shale.
The poetry of petrification.

That T-Rex skull hasn't been bone for millions of years,
But it's here.

Memory without language.
Art without intent.

It's all still here.

Pub

As a young American with Irish ancestry,
my romanticized Ireland was a place where even in dive bars they love
poetry.

Sticky floors and Seamus Heaney.

I've never been to Ireland.

And I've come to distrust white America's talk of ancestry,
but the internet is certainly a dive bar

and there's enough poetry carved into the back booths
to keep me romantic.

Epitaph

Our bodies have died many times.

These aren't the cells you were born with.
A new skin each month.
Neuroplasticity building the plane mid-flight.

We in the pilot's chairs are already ghosts.
Here and not here.
Built of memories the way a beach is built of sand.

Shifting.
Ships anchored to fog.

To live is to haunt.

Kin

If you've ever grabbed a stick
from the ground and thought "oh, this is a good stick,"
then we're family.

The Ache

When we feel pained or drained by the ugliness in the world,
it is because we are mourning.
We mourn for our love of what the world could be,
for a place that isn't here, but should be.

That pain is the overwhelming goodness in you hungering for an echo
of itself.
What is. What was. What could be.

It is a terrible mark of honor to mourn.
It means we have the courage to love
in an imperfect, impermanent world.

It means we sided with difficult tenderness
over numbing indifference.

An Honest Appraisal

You are good enough and your worth isn't dependent on your
achievements.

It's not just an affirmation.
It's true.

It seems like your worth is based on your achievements
in much the same way it seems like the sun is made of fire.

Both are common sense.
Both are incorrect.

Common sense is common because at first glance it appears true,
not because it actually is.

We build complex lives,
but if you're feeling lost or trapped,
look to your foundations and make sure this basic truth
is there in the stone.

You are good enough and your worth isn't dependent on your
achievements.

What achievements could two-year-old-you claim?
Were you worthless then?
So, what has changed?

Expectation?
Whose expectations?

Let's say achievements are partly built from your worth.

Okay.

They are also part luck, and context, and timing, and happenstance, and privilege, and opportunity,
and the subjective priorities of the people defining "achievement" for this year/place/culture/community.

Be proud of your achievements.
But understand that they are not your worth.
They are too far beyond our control to be as fundamental as worth.

Two-year-old-you didn't earn their worth.

It was innate then. It is innate now.

It doesn't grow or diminish because of shifting fortunes or expectations.

Your worth is an essential, untouchable part of you.

You are a rare and magnificent thinking, feeling being. You make your home on a deeply uncommon planet in a staggering, vast universe.

You are the planet. You are the universe.

Do you think any of that is touched by test scores? By bank accounts? By job titles? By possessions?

No.

You are good enough and your worth isn't dependent on your achievements.

Geography

You are a flesh and bone animal,
a landscape of biological wonders

hosting a billion unique memories like a nation of phantoms.

We can be measured, but never mapped.

Our minds are half window and half mirror.

I will never be wise enough to know when I'm looking out
or when I'm looking in.

Telltale

The human heart pumps 2,000 gallons of blood a day, but if you try to ask it where all that blood came from, it will get very defensive.

Illogical

We all step away from the data.

The paved road of facts tapers to a dirt track beneath our feet,
a muddy deer path through the brambles.
The trees lean in.

"Life is short and uncomfortable. Why bother putting on socks?
Why make the coffee?"

Science can't answer this for you. Not without your help.
A what is not a why.
A how is not a why.
But whatever you answer,
will be correct.

Can you feel the weight of it?

Be careful.
Be thoughtful.
Answer kindly.

What you decide
matters.

Grudge

It turns out,
everyone you dislike is tumbling along the stream of time,
bumping and rolling through the oddities of life
on their way to sleep and echoes,

so you are now free to focus on other concerns.

Regroup

You lend your strength to justice.
You hold in tears.
You carry anxiety like an ember on your palm.

The hungry seas of human affairs churn beneath your boat.

Come ashore for a day.
Touch something green.
Let the whispering life in you speak to nature
and find its voice renewed.

Simple

Moss is 300 million years old.

At home on every continent.

No deep roots,
no towering trunks,

yet it tasted the air before the first feather,
before shrews stirred the leaf litter.

Moss doesn't race trees skyward hunting for sunlight.
It thrives just the same.

When your mind hisses like a kettle,
look to your elders, to the green lessons

of soft, simple quiet beneath the sun.

Look Again

See a bird and dismiss it.
See a bird and learn its name.
See a bird and study its behavior.
See a bird and question the physics of flight.
See a bird and trace its DNA back to the dinosaurs.
Life can pass over us unnoticed or be rich in poetry.

I know it isn't easy.
It's hard to slow down.
It's hard to make time for questions,
harder still to make room for answers.
Some days, I'm too tired to look again,
to look closer.

And yet, each year I stumble into this fact.
Curiosity is worth the effort.

Apologies #1

When you are a crab scuttling along the seabed,
the ocean is your sky and the whales
are your clouds.

It is majestic,
ancient and vast,
cathedral and cradle,
but you tell no one because...

you're a little shellfish.

Devotion

The moon loves her moths.

Not for beauty or deeds.
Not for vespers sung in a fluttering
like night-wind in the wheat,

scales drifting like shattered starlight.

It's because, without word or thought,
their bodies seek her out in the airy darkness.
It's what they are,
love without decision.

Instinctual adoration.

Reflection

The danger in trying to hide who you are is that you'll succeed, and you'll start to see a stranger in the mirror of other people.

Let's

Let's be exhausted together.
Let's laugh about it.
Let's clasp each other like two strangers
who just saw a horror pass by.
Let's ugly cry over the sink.
Let's eat the baking chocolate.
Let's meet-up without a plan.
Let's love what's broken.
Let's be beautiful in defeat and reckless with trust.
Let's be stubbornly soft.
Let's be human.

Important if True

I don't know who needs to hear this,
but there is a river of molten spiders deep within the Earth that dreams
of your face.

That river would seek you out if not for the strong bedrock
that keeps it contained.

One day, the stone may fail,
then we'll know who needed to hear this.

Just Words on a Page

Nature isn't a poem.
It's your breath.
It's the curve of your ribs.
It's the dance of galaxies like pollen on the wind.
It's fire and frost and violet buds.
It's coral like cities of bone in a dream of blue.
It's the machinery of memory and a lightning scar
on a cemetery oak.
Nature isn't a poem.

101

Some days,
language is a net.

Or a bucket.

Or a teaspoon.

Meaning often lands on a texture spectrum from puddle-water
to mashed potatoes.

Language and meaning.

These two ideas interact somehow.

You could sculpt a dachshund.
Or just splash out a rhythm.

Splash.
Splash.
Splash.

Anyway, that sums up writing.

Class dismissed.

Tired of Forever

Fantasies of immortality are toxic because
they are fantasies of sameness.

As if the point of life is only to be here,
piling up breaths like coins in a dragon's horde.

If I lived another thousand years,
it would be a tragedy if I were anything less
than a stranger to myself today.

Is that immortality?

Some say they don't want all the time,
just more.

A question of degree.

A snooze button for impermanence.

Children often suppose becoming an adult will solve their problems.
They will be bigger.
Stronger.
A flexible bedtime.

A question of degree.

Does adulthood banish problems?

Compared to many creatures, we are already long lived.
Stand next to a honeybee.
Measure yourself against it.
Now you're ancient and powerful.

Are you satisfied?

The true unit of our vital, present consciousness is the moment.
This moment.
Not the year. Not the decade. Not the eon.
The moment.

This moment is who we are.
An instant that blooms and fades.
More of them will not equal more of you.

I know the things I love about myself do not exist solely within me.
I don't need to trap them in stasis beyond time, walled-off and lifeless.
They will not be lost when I return to the effortless unity of nature.

They are of nature, the things I treasure.

The good in me awoke through natural processes.
Those processes continue.
Those processes hold what I love in trust.

They hold you as well.

We borrow all that we are, all that we admire, from this flawed,
temporary, beautiful world.

Forever is the otherness we crave when we grow frustrated
with what is.
The greener grass.
It is a stranger who, unmet, can remain full of potential. Endlessly,
pleasantly hypothetical.

It isn't a character flaw to wish for forever. It's born of love. A love so
strong we would break reality to hold onto it.

Just remember this:

Nothing we know or value was born of forever.

They were born of change. They arose from impermanence.

Change.
Impermanence.

These things aren't our enemies.
They don't hate us.
They opened the path to all we are.

Smoke

If you've ever smelled woodsmoke near a forest at night,
then you've met a ghost,

a memory walking outside a mind,
calling to its kin within yours.

Feel that tingle of recognition?
Your memories are answering,

tracing the pale threads
through the dark woods,

stitching firefly summers in your head
to flames you'll never see.

Be Ready

The moon has been circling us for a very long time.

Soon, it will pounce.

Eavesdropping

Trees are the way we listen in on the conversation
between cosmic energy and earthly matter.

The sun posed a question.
I didn't quite catch it.

Something about hearing all motion as music.
Something about galaxies stretching their joints after cramped quarters.
Something about vastness as a love language.

Not all questions are made of words.
Some are tides of heat and light.
Some change the listener before they can answer.

The Earth took its time.
Of course it did.
A question as kind as sunlight
deserves an answer as generous as trees.

Definitions

Soil.
Air.
Sea.

Basic words for complex things.

Language is amazing,
but it compresses huge, messy concepts
into tidy signifiers like overstuffed pockets.

Unpack the common words.
See what's hiding inside.

Stone.
Sun.
Tree.

Not simple.
Fundamental.
Each, an invitation.

Foundational

The inert mass of the Earth
is as much an architect of our lives as air and water.

The pull of those trillions of tons of rock
shaped every aspect of our bodies.

The salt in our blood.
The strength of our bones.

We often celebrate the sunlight.
Don't forget the stone.

Imposter

When the creeping doubts come, I like to remind myself —

feeling like a fake is evidence that I respect my chosen endeavor
so much
that I fear I'll fail to honor it.

Seems like a pretty good sign I'm on the right path.

Sparse

Winter is landscape poetry.

A white page.

A scribbled elm on a snow hill.

The empty space makes each syllable of life

vital.

Prickly

When in doubt,
let nature guide you.

Specifically, cactuses.

Be still.
Stay hydrated.
Shelter owls.
Stab your predators.

It's that easy.

Vantage

In a bright blue noon,
when cloud shadows swim the streets like carp,
the sun is a promise.

In a dark velvet night,
when the moon hints at a blaze in exile,
the sun is a secret.

In each case, the sun has not changed.
We have.

Options

The rat will adapt to most any landscape.

The beaver will gnaw and slap and drag the landscape to fit her needs.

I can't tell you which is better.

Just reminding you that both are options.

Look there.

Beyond the parking lot.

Past the broken pallets and sun-bleached Coors cans.
Down where the march of saplings meets the ditch lilies.

A deer.

You know this won't last.

You know the sight wasn't arranged just for you,
that it isn't nature's message of quiet wholeness,
that the deer didn't arrive because you needed it to.

And yet.
And yet.
And yet.

You suspect it will. It was. It is. It did.

And with just a little effort,
you'll be right.

Foxfire

In the dark woods,
I look to the rotting stump,
a heap of shadow,
a tombstone castle in the leaf litter.

There are lights in the windows.

The foxfire is awake tonight.
Fungi and wood staying up past the oak's lifetime
to tell stories of phantoms in deep waters.
Bioluminescence.

Morning Talk

My arm brushed a blue spruce on a gray hike.

It spoke in a voice made of sparrows,
stinging the quiet like sparks from a kicked fire.

That sudden sound hung a question on the air,
but I did not answer.

I knew that to answer would end a discussion
I dearly want to stretch on
for a lifetime.

Business Model

Trees arise from dirt and rain.
Sun and thoughtless understanding.

They awaken with all they need to stand,
unsheltered,
beneath the open sky for hundreds of years.

They make their livings without tools or flame,
without a spoken phrase or a written word.

Their colleagues, their technologies,
the pollinators,
the forging birds,
the industrious squirrels,

are profitable and unexploited.

Are effective and uncoerced.

They succeed while giving more than they gain.

Whatever wonders we create,
whatever distant worlds we may visit,
will forever be a byproduct

of the virtue of trees.

Passport

My citizenship is American.
But, my ancestry is Irish and Scandinavian.
But, my humanity is from Africa.
But, my life awoke in the sea.
But, the sea coalesced on a young Earth.
But, the Earth was shaped by the touch of the sun.
But, the sun was born to the forces of the universe.
But, it all once knew the unity of the singularity.
And it still does.

Fan Fic

A pine tree is a shaggy coat
and an elven fortress
and a monument to wind
and the sun's embassy on Earth
and a summer tower besieged by frost
and every one of them is simultaneously the best tree I've ever seen.

Resolution

I give up wanting to be whole.
To be strong.
To be beyond criticism.

Instead,
I will be creative with my empathy.
I will not curse my flaws.
I will live in the light of honest vulnerability.

I will look at a sculpture and understand
that need is what calls art from bare stone.
Perfection calls to nothing.

Not to brag.

Hey.
We're humans.
A pretty young species.
You've probably heard of us.
We're the top lifeform on Earth.
You can tell because smart phones and toilets and such.

Sure, we need older creatures to make all our food and oxygen,
but that's all.
Oh, and we need them to live in our guts to help us digest things,
but it's not a big deal.

We're on top.
We know because we've said so.

Oh, we're also the smartest.
That's important.

"Smart" is a word we invented using our smarts.
It's a measure of how well any creature
can do things humans value
via methods we understand.
Simple, right?

I assure you,
we're very smart.
And very in charge.

Away Message

I'm away from my desk.
The desk itself is barely there,
its fixity is a fiction we hang on fluttering atoms riding tectonic plates
atop a whirling planet orbiting a cosmic inferno that races through the
galaxy at 200 kilometers per second.

Also, I'll have limited email access.

Poetic License

There are sensible criticisms of viewing nature
through poetic comparison.

The Earth, its complex web of interconnected life,
its tons of molten stone, its invisible pull of gravity,
of magnetism, is not literally our mother.

Yet also,
it is.

Every facet of our species is shaped
by the physical and chemical characteristics of Earth.

Calling the Earth our mother is a concise route
to an overarching truth. It's an accessible way to describe
a complex concept. That's the virtue of metaphor.

The drawback would be in using poetics
to shut down curiosity, study, or specificity.

To say, "the Earth is our mother, so
let's close the book on geology, chemistry, and biology."

This would be a misuse of art. This would be painting
a landscape over a window.

We need the poetic lens because quantifying
the physical properties of iron isn't quite the same
as weighing the significance of how the iron in our blood
connects us to the planet beneath our feet,
to the heat of ancient stars.

Plain fact isn't always the best ambassador of truth
or our surest route to meaning.

Bloom

Poems are like flowers.
They draw your eye to something beautiful,
but they remain creatures of rain and soil.

The work to lift a violet into the light happens down in the dark.

Each bright petal marks the passing of a hundred earthworms.

If your creative process feels like a mess,
you're in good company.

Clergy

Vultures are holy creatures.
Tending the dead.
Bowing low.
Bared head.
Whispers to cold flesh,
"Your old name is not your king.
I rename you 'Everything.'"

Covenant

I know a rotting stump near a broken fence.
It is alive in so many ways that have nothing to do with the tree it once
was and everything to do with the tree it once was.

That's the friendship of life and death.
Death teaches life about unity.
Life shelters death from forever.

Impractical

I'm not needed here.
Acorns aren't needed,
nor white-throated sparrows.

Our not-quite-round Earth isn't needed.
All of us needlessly disturbing the polite nothing
of the neighborhood.

Yet, here we are.
And need had no say in it.

So, as in art and kindness,
perhaps needlessness knows best.

Make things.

Make things that might embarrass you.

Make things that leave you feeling exposed,
like you've left a vital part of yourself out on the line to dry.

Make things that pester you with growing pains
as you lie down to sleep.

Make things with the kind of love you can't ever take back.

Partnership

It's frankly ridiculous that we can't find one species of moss that will live on my head and eat anxiety and depression.

Stylish, functional symbiosis.

Have we really looked everywhere?

The Return

A human wondering about death is like a snowflake considering its fall toward the sea.

The fear is in losing the self,
the stark distinction of crystalline borders.

The comfort is in seeking to remember the absolute unity of the water below.

We could name each mote of snow and mourn its loss when
it reaches the sea,
but we understand that the water was neither lost nor diminished
by the journey.

Close Enough

Sunlight becomes a leaf.

The leaf nourishes a caterpillar.

The caterpillar feeds a bird.

The bird flies too high and is gobbled up by the sun.

The bird becomes sunlight.

This is the circle of life.

Lineage

The new green leaf of an ancient oak.
Tender.
Gone in the autumn.
What does it have to do with all those tons of wood below?

Count twelve generations back
and you have over 4,000 grandparents.

To say the leaf is soft and fleeting is not the true story of a thing
distilled from a billion weathered storms.

The leaf is one season.
The leaf is a forest of years.

Hush

Be careful.

If you hold a shell up to your ear,
you can hear the ocean,

but the ocean can hear you back.

Zoom #2

Dear Team,

In lieu of our Zoom meeting this afternoon,
let's all agree to wander beneath the trees tonight when
the moon is high.

Let's sink our fingers into the soil and send messages
via fungi and salamander.
If that fails, let's simply live on,

having lost nothing at all.

Knowing

We are not how the universe knows itself.

We are how humans know the universe.

Words and thoughts are *our* way of knowing,
not *the* way of knowing.

Translating a mountain into a word,
into a measurement,
does not bring new knowledge into the world.

It brings new knowledge into us.

The mountain was perfectly in touch with its own wholeness
without neurons, without language,
without learning our name for it.

We may have spotted the shores of understanding
from our small boat,
but that doesn't mean we conjured them from the sea.

Flock

Humans are atom shepherds,
tending our bodies.
Flocks of cells coaxed into action.
One day, our sheep will go,
and in pastures of flowers or stars,
they will wear our gentle touches
like ivy woven into their wool.
Let them walk with our blessing
to the green hills of ever after.

Perhaps

Down in the soil beneath your ribs,
a single acorn sleeps.

Warm and smooth as coffee with cream.

Perhaps it will never be an oak drinking in 100 feet of sky.

It doesn't matter.

What matters is that it might.
You might.

And that potential sings in your bones
like rain on stone.

Risk and Reward

Feeling deeply is dangerous.

Doing anything else is tragic.

Middle Years

Matter.

Energy.

Neither created nor destroyed.

You were there. In the beginning.

When all that is scattered like starlings.

You will be there. In the end.

When the gentle quiet collects like dew.

What is there to fear?

A Kiss

I feel your presence here
like the smell of pine in the dark,

a word of cool air on the tongue,
soft green fingers brushing your throat,

near as skin and very much alive.

Meet me there,
beneath the tangle of hemlock skirts

and we'll add our breath to their sweet memories.

Crop

Meaning does not ripen out in the fields.
It doesn't swell into sweetness beneath the sun.

You won't pluck it from a branch,
won't find it tumbled whole and waiting in the grass.

It ripens inside your skull,
in the light of your intention.

What you crave is uniquely yours.
Look inward.

Flow

Lives aren't completed.
They're concluded.

You are, and forever will be, unfinished.
This is nature.
Cycles and spectrums.
Moments and seasons.

Do you ask when the weather will be complete?
The spring finished?

Your life won't have one point or purpose.
You're lovelier than that.

Just Because

Write poetry because you need to.

Because it's hard.

Because language is broken,
but if you brave the sharp edges,

you might make something worth having.

Oracle

In the center of the forest,
there is an unlikely stone that remembers when the mountains
were new.

It waits in a circle of moss like the pupil of a green eye.

You kneel and ask it a wordless question.

It answers.

"Cherish exactly who you are. For there can never be another."

Compliments for Humans:

"For a thing so full of blood, it's amazing you don't slosh when you walk."

"Three breath-holes? Now you're just showing off."

"The way you move makes it hard to believe you're stuffed with bones."

"Wow, that's a lot of skin, but you really make it work."

Horizon

If we wait until the world is perfect before allowing ourselves to smile,
we'll be waiting forever.

That horizon will continue to be out of reach
even if we skip lunch to walk toward it.

Life is happening here,
where our breath rejoins the wind,

not at the far limit of our sight.

Until Next Time

There's an old tradition of loaning something to a friend when you visit so you'll have an excuse to meet again.

It reminds me of all that I've borrowed.
The iron in my blood.
The air in my lungs.
The flowing water of life.

When we borrow from a friend, the returning is not a chore.
It's a reunion.

Hello Traveler

Greet yourself as you would a stranger walking in a circle of honey-colored lantern light through a hushed and watchful forest.

My thanks to you, wanderer, who walks in open defiance of this world's dangers in order to meet its many wonders.

Gratitude, brave soul.

One of the wonders is you.

Sate

One thought is always hungry.
"I'm not being productive enough."

We must bundle these words in an old blanket
and sit them by a fire on a crisp night.

We must heal them with wordless wind and smoke.

We must do the same for the culture that made their hunger terrible.

Perspective

You can send your thoughts waltzing through the centuries.
You can make a warm drink the prize of a lifetime.

You can imagine the Earth as a firefly speck in an ink black sky.
You can make any simple kindness the essential truth of your story.

See with intention.

Collection

Collect objects infused with stories.
Buy a hand-carved wooden spoon.

Rescue and refinish a table.
Hang someone's art on your walls.

It doesn't need to be costly,
just rich in story.

Save yourself from the feeling that you're sinking
beneath the bulk of gray, lifeless products.

Many things are made with love, with care,
with intention.

Some purchases make us consumers,
some make us a community.

Recycled

I think if you lived for eons
and saw how it all rearranges
and transforms
again and again and again,

eventually you would realize
that inherent in the act of loving one thing
is a love for all things.

The whole,
absurd jumble of it all,
each and every atom touched with adoration.

Apologies #2

The adults of most moth species don't have mouths,
but you can help.

Donate your mouth to a moth in need.

Remember, the difference between "moth" and "mouth"

is U.

Legend

An acorn is carried off to be eaten.
Now or ten million years ago.
It's forgotten.
It's bitten by winter.
It sinks into spring.
It stands and thrives,
tender and hard,
on bare earth, storms, and starlight for 300 years.
I sit. I breathe. I write it all down.
I live off the sighs of giants.

Sidenotes:

The most haunted house is still less creepy than the least haunted cornfield.

The sky sings in wrens and swears in seagulls.

Blankets are overachieving nets.

High school is not the best years of your life.

Geese should be reclassified as weather.

Eating maple syrup makes you a Tree-Dracula.

Every castle is a sandcastle eventually.

Forsythia

As forsythia grows tall,
its branches bend beneath their own weight,
bowing to the ground in arches of yellow flowers.

Wherever they touch the earth,
the branches root again and send up new shoots,
stitching gold across the landscape.

Some new kinds of knowledge shift our center of gravity,
staggering us,
bending us low beneath the burden.

If you think of your worldview as a stone tower,
this shift is a cataclysm of splintered rock.

If your worldview is forsythia,
then every startling truth that bends you low becomes a new connection
to the earth,
a new way to stand,
an invitation to grow.

We live in a time of strong wind and sudden pressure.
It is not an age for towers.

It's an age for stubborn flowers.

About the Author:

Jarod K. Anderson lives in a white house between a forest and a graveyard. He writes and narrates The CryptoNaturalist podcast, a scripted audio drama about a folksy narrator exploring bizarre places and impossible wildlife. You can find more of Jarod's writing in places like *Asimov's, Escape Pod,* and *Apex Magazine.*

Author Website: www.jarodkanderson.com

The CryptoNaturalist: Available anywhere you find podcasts or stream directly from our website.
www.cryptonaturalist.com

Twitter: @CryptoNature

Facebook: /CryptoNaturalist

Instagram: @CryptoNaturalist

To support Jarod's work and gain access to exclusive content, visit Patreon.com/CryptoNaturalist

Made in the USA
Las Vegas, NV
16 December 2022

63099678R10055